Praise f

"As an author, you invest hundreds, if not thousands, of hours in crafting your story into written words, enough words to make it a book. Then you realize that this book could become even more alive as an audio version. But whom to add this dimension? Enter Richard Rieman, a man who has dedicated his working life to breathing life into the words of others.

When I went looking for the right person to narrate and produce my audiobook, I was lucky that Richard was one of more than 30 who auditioned, and that I selected him. Most importantly, with Richard as my alter ego reading aloud my memoir, he faithfully reflected my enthusiasm, wonderment, pride, humility, fascination, and all those other emotions that make my story what it is.

I feel blessed to have had Richard Rieman read and produce my audiobook."

— Bruce Comstock,
Author of *A Life in the Air*

"As an author, I've worked with Richard on eight projects now and he's done a great job on all of them. What I really like is the way he can add a little laugh, or something similar to a smile, at just the right time. It brings the book to life and makes you want to keep listening.

Trust me. I've listened to dozens of auditions, from so called voice artists—most of them are flat and dry, and would just put you to sleep. Listen to one of Richard's books, and you'll see he's nothing like that. He can make your words leap off the page and encourage listeners to purchase more of your works."

— Nick Vulich, Author of *eBay 2015*
and *Killing President Lincoln*

"Richard, I'm currently putting the final touches on *The Treaty of Nine* series and I wanted to say, WOW! Hearing your reading again has just blown me away. It's fantastic. You've done such an awesome job and it's a huge motivator to get me back to writing full time so I can hear you bring more characters to life."

— Adam Train, Author of *Transcendent Tales*

"It was an absolute pleasure working with Richard Rieman to produce my audiobook. Richard is very professional and is a great communicator. He guided me through the process step by step. He has a wonderful voice and his narration of *SHOT DOWN* could not have been better."

— Steve Snyder, Author of *SHOT DOWN*

The Author's Guide to AudioBook Creation

RICHARD RIEMAN

AuthorYOU Mini-Guide Series

THE AUTHOR'S GUIDE TO AUDIOBOOK CREATION
by Richard Rieman

© Copyright 2016 by Richard Rieman

Books may be purchased by contacting the publisher and author
at: Richard@RRVoice.com

Publishers: Breckenridge Press and Mile High Press
Cover and Interior Design: Nick Zelinger (NZGraphics.com)
Editors: Judith Briles (TheBookShepherd.com)
and John Maling (EditingByJohn.com)
Book Consulting: Judith Briles (The Book Shepherd)

Library of Congress Catalog Number: 2015920781
ISBN: 978-0-9971002-0-4 (print)
ISBN: 978-0-9971002-1-1 (e-book)

Reference | Publishing | Audio Books

First Edition   Printed in the USA

Foreword

Ideas get birthed from a variety of places. *The Author's Guide to AudioBook Creation* is no different. Richard Rieman showed up one Saturday morning in July at the monthly AuthorYOU Circles I offer to aspiring and already published authors in Denver, Colorado. (Summertime usually finds our authoring group on my back deck).

Listening to him share what he did, how he did it, and then asking a variety questions led me to ask him: "Tell me more about what you do." As a river of information flowed forth, I immediately knew four things:

1. I would hire him to create an audiobook of my latest mini-guide, *The CrowdFunding Guide for Authors & Writers* (something I hadn't even considered doing);

2. I wanted him to do a program for the AuthorU.org community ... his years of experience in voice work and moxie of the audiobook side of production would deliver essential tips, tricks and how-tos;

3. Several of my Book Shepherding clients needed his services and I would make immediate introductions; and

4. He needed to write a book for authors and I would be his Book Shepherd.

Within a few months, my audiobook was completed. None of it would have been accomplished without Richard at the helm. He was referred to clients who in turn were equally elated with their results. A special program was created for the AuthorU community in both in-person presentation and webinar and the fourth goal ... *The Author's Guide to AudioBook Creation* is now in your hands. Check – Check – Check – and Check!

One of the things that Richard brings to you is his depth of experience. If you are considering being your own voice, you will get an honest assessment from his years at both the mic as an on-air personality and as a voice editor as to whether your voice is a right fit for an audiobook. If not, he will refer you to someone who is, or do it himself if he is. After all, he's voiced characters from a pirate to an alien; from a bottlegger to a cowboy; among many other characters, including accents as well. You just might find that he has the perfect delivery, style and tone for your story.

The other thing that I love is his professionalism. He lines up everything needed; keeps the author and other players on track; gets the right studio team in place and finally guides you through the final stages of production including placement so buyers can get a copy.

If you are considering creating an audiobook— whether you are the voice or you hire a professional narrator—*The Author's Guide to AudioBook Creation* is the essential companion you need. You will get the critical elements on what steps you need to take; how to engage a narrator (and what to avoid); what costs to expect; how to produce your audiobook; a variety of resources; how to work with Amazon and ACX and other providers; and of course, plenty of tips and tricks of the trade.

I'm thankful that Richard Rieman opened the audiobook door for me. And I'm honored to have his book within the series.

Get ready for the next evolution of your book ... and join the audiobook revolution.

Judith Briles, The Book Shepherd

Author of *The CrowdFunding Guide for Authors & Writers* and *AuthorYOU: Your Guide to Book Publishing*

CONTENTS

THE AUDIOBOOK REVOLUTION

© TheBookShepherd.com

Telling Your Story

I've been a pirate, a cowboy, a bootlegger, six aliens, two monsters, a world famous balloon pilot, and a B-17 bomber pilot shot down in WWII. I've traveled to other times, dimensions, mysterious islands and haunted houses. I've helped you sell stuff on eBay and self-publish your Kindle book. I've been a man who lost 150 pounds, and l have lived forever.

Who am I really? I'm Richard Rieman, and I am an audiobook narrator. I'm a performer in the theater of the mind.

Since the age of seven, I've been a professional writer. I discovered that if I wrote stories that included the names of my second grade classmates (on a ruled piece of paper, both sides, in pencil), they would give me five cents to read them. Bingo! Now I had comic book money.

When I narrate an audiobook, I quietly tell you in your headphones:

> *Listen to me, I have something important-interesting-dramatic-funny-entertaining-wonderful to tell you!*

People primarily listen in cars, but they are now listening to audiobooks on their smartphones while exercising, or doing mindless chores and multitasking.

Why should you do an audiobook? Become part of the AudioBook Revolution!

Compared to Amazon's twenty-five million plus titles, Amazon's audiobook sales company Audible has just 170,000 audiobooks available. In the next five years, Amazon expects that number to grow to more than one million audiobooks.

You might think e-books are the fastest growing book publishing format. Nope! In fact, e-book growth has stagnated since 2014. Audiobooks are by far the fastest growing way people enjoy books. It's the hot ticket for today's author.

You're an author. Should you have an audiobook as well as an e-book, paperback, or hardcover?

In one word: Absolutely. And I will show you how.

Why You Should Grab Your Readers by the Ears

Almost half (46 percent) of people say they have listened to an audiobook. Why? Audiobook buyers love the convenience of listening, especially on those long car trips or commutes. The average American work commute is about 50 minutes each day, or just over four hours a week, and it's getting longer every year!

People primarily listen in cars, but they are now listening to audiobooks on their smartphones while exercising, or doing mindless chores and multitasking. If that doesn't get your attention, here are more numbers for you. In 2015, the annual Audio Publishers Association (APA) survey reported a 20 percent increase in audiobook sales compared to 6 percent for e-books and just over a 4 percent increase in sales in the overall book trade industry. For 2016, the APA estimates that audiobook annual sales will total more than $2 billion dollars. Will you get your share?

It is Marketing 101 to be everywhere your readers (and buyers) are. AudioBook buyers are a different source of readers. AudioBooks are a new revenue stream for your already created book. With minimal upfront expense, the royalties can come in for years.

New technologies such as Amazon's "Whispersync" feature allows readers to seamlessly move from the digital version to the audiobook, picking up in the place the reader left off.

The cost of recording an audiobook has fallen from around $25,000 in the late 1990s, when most audiobooks were recorded in major LA and New York City studios, to less than $3,000 now, thanks to the explosion of home recording studios.

Acclaimed science fiction and fantasy author
Neil Gaiman, said on his blog at *NeilGaiman.com:*

> *At the heart of the system is this idea:*
> *The rights to an audiobook often remain*
> *unrealized and the book is never recorded.*
> *And there's huge potential sitting there,*
> *too—the potential for creative work, the*
> *potential for new income, and the potential*
> *for good listening.*

In Stephen King's memoir, *On Writing*, he credits
his decades-long obsession with audiobooks
with sharpening his prose, improving the pacing
of his narratives and helping him ward off lazy
phrases and clichés. In the summer of 2015,
King released a new short story, *Drunken*
Fireworks, as an audiobook exclusive, months
before the story arrived in print. King believes
that it will turn more of his readers into
audiobook converts.

The late great author and writing coach Gary Provost in *100 Ways to Improve Your Writing* says reading your written words out loud will make you a better writer:

> *This sentence has five words. Here are five more words.*

> *Five-word sentences are fine. But several together become monotonous. Listen to what is happening. The writing is getting boring. The sound of it drones. It's like a stuck record. The ear demands some variety.*

> *Now listen. I vary the sentence length, and I create music. Music. The writing sings. It has a pleasant rhythm, a lilt, a harmony. I use short sentences. And I use sentences of medium length. And sometimes, when I am certain the reader is rested, I will engage him with a sentence of considerable length, a sentence that burns with the energy and builds with all the impetus of a crescendo,*

*the roll of the drums, the crash of the
cymbals—sounds that say listen to this, it
is important.*

*So write with a combination of short,
medium and long sentences. Create a sound
that pleases the reader's ear. Don't just
write words. Write music.*

Audible has more than 30 original audio works
and more in the pipeline. The first was *The
Starling Project* narrated by Alfred Molina with a
full cast. It was written by thriller writer Jeffery
Deaver, turning his bestseller into a compelling
radio drama beyond just another book.

And there's the audio listening experience itself.
You may think you have read Harry Potter, but if
you listen to the brilliant narrator Jim Dale, J.K.
Rowling's universe will come alive in an incredible
way her books and the movies didn't, and
couldn't, capture.

10 Crazy (but True) Things about AudioBooks

1. The first audiobooks were called "Talking Books" and were created in the 1930s for people with visual disabilities in America and Britain. This group included war-blinded soldiers and blind civilians who couldn't read braille.

2. The first full-length talking books were on LP (long-playing) vinyl records and included the Bible, the Declaration of Independence, and Shakespeare.

3. It was illegal for sighted persons to listen to LP audiobooks from 1934 until 1948, because publishers and authors' unions controlling royalties and rights did not want them made available for public sale. They might cut into book sales!

4. Libraries are still a major source of audiobooks, accounting for more than 40 percent of audiobook listening, primarily through "Books on Tape," which is now part of Penguin Random House.

5. Thousands of libraries also lend digital audiobooks through *OneClickdigital*, a division of Recorded Books, or the *OverDrive app*, which allows library patrons to download audiobooks to their devices.

6. Complete, unabridged audiobooks can still require up to 15 CDs.

7. Road travelers can buy a Books-On-Audio CD at Cracker Barrel restaurants. When you're done, you return it to a Cracker Barrel at another location for a new audiobook and get a refund minus a small handling fee.

8. Android and iPhone audible apps have a feature that allows you to speed up the narration to between 1.5 and 3 times normal narrating speed, something visually-impaired readers do every day.

9. Jim Dale, who narrated the *Harry Potter* series, is in the Guinness Book of World Records for the 146 separate voices he created for *Harry Potter and the Deathly Hallows.*

10. Audible invented and commercialized the first digital audio player in 1997. The device is currently in the Smithsonian.

The Top 10 Audiobook Genres

More than 75 percent of audiobooks are made up of "made up" stuff—fiction. The top-selling audiobook genres on Amazon's *Audible.com* are:

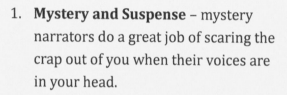

1. **Mystery and Suspense** – mystery narrators do a great job of scaring the crap out of you when their voices are in your head.

2. **Bestsellers** – guess what? Sell a lot of books and people will buy the audiobook too!

3. **Science Fiction and Fantasy** – there are times we all would rather be someplace else in time or space, and the audio versions beam us there.

4. **History and Biographies** – Napoleon Bonaparte said, "History is a set of lies that people have agreed upon." And this way, narrators can lie to you.

5. **Business and Self-Improvement** – multitaskers of the world unite by powering up "down time" with information on improving their lives.

6. **Children and Young Adult** – the Audio Publishers Association's study shows 36% of audiobook listeners buy children's or young adult audiobooks, and increasingly popular choice.

7. **Inspiration and Religion** – a good audiobook narrator can take you to church.

8. **Erotica/Romance** – only 10 percent of audiobook sales, but the popularity of *Fifty Shades of Grey* has led to a rising

interest in erotica and "romance" with differing degrees of blush inducement. A full 25 percent of the titles listed as available for audio production on ACX, the Audiobook Creation Exchange, are in the Erotica/Romance categories.

9. **Sports** – especially fantasy football, where we are losing a generation to fake football competitions.

10. **Westerns** – because there is a little cowboy or cowgirl in each of us.

Toughest books to translate to audio—photography books, cookbooks, textbooks, and language instruction. Let's face it, some books are just not meant to be read aloud.

Make sure you retain
your audio rights.
You, not an outside publisher,
should have them!

② GETTING STARTED

Demand Your (Audio) Rights!

Let's jump right in with step one in getting your audiobook produced.

Confirm you have the audio rights for your book by checking your print or e-book contract with

your publisher to see if you have retained
the audio rights, so you can go ahead with
audiobook production without the publisher
taking any of the royalties.

If you're self-published (say, through Kindle
Direct Publishing, CreateSpace or IngramSpark),
you have the audio rights.

If you do **not** have audio rights, and the current
rights holder has not produced an audiobook
of your work, you may want to start the rights
reversion process, requesting them to be
reverted to your name alone.

The following is an example of an audiobook
rights reversion clause you can request be
inserted in your book publishing contract
(or added as an addendum):

> If the Publisher does not either exercise
> or license audio recording rights to any
> Work within 60 days from the date of the
> Publisher's initial publication of such

Work, the Author may request in writing
that the Publisher revert to the Author
such rights, and the Publisher shall revert
such rights to such Work within 30 days of
stated request in writing.

Make sure you retain your audio rights. You, not
an outside publisher, should have them!

The Different Worlds of AudioBook Publishing

There are the Superpowers, the Independents,
the Specialty Publishers, and the 900-pound
Gorilla.

The Superpowers

The way it used to be, actors who recorded
books worked exclusively in professional
recording studios. They were guided in their
performances by audiobook directors and
given technical support by professional sound

engineers. That still happens, but getting an audiobook produced at the biggest publishers is just as hard, if not harder, than getting a book published in print. Publishers base their decision on the potential market value of the book, and the bestsellers in the print world will always get preference.

The big publishers prefer to work with agents, especially those they know, rather than directly with the author. A Superpower publisher will rarely re-publish a self-published audiobook, but if it has sold well, it can happen.

As an example of a Superpower, Penguin Random House has 12 recording studios and producers on both the East and West coasts. Penguin produces between 700 and 800 titles annually, about a fourth of what it publishes on the print side. Each audiobook featuring a top Hollywood film star or big name in the audiobook narration world can cost $30,000 or more to produce.

The Superpowers of audiobook publishing include Penguin Random House, Hachette Audio (formerly Time Warner Audio books), Harper-Collins (Harlequin) Audio, MacMillan Audio, Recorded Books, Simon & Schuster Audio, and Amazon's Audible.

Why did Amazon
buy Audible and create ACX?
Because Amazon wants to
sell more books in any format
and recognizes the rising
growth trajectory
of audiobooks.

The Independents

Independent Audio Publishers vary in size, with larger studios like Brilliance, Blackstone, Podium Publishing, and Deyan Audio producing hundreds of audiobooks annually. Deyan Audio has two locations and owns nine recording booths and employs more than 100 editors and engineers, along with 30 directors.

There are smaller audiobook production opportunities in cities across the country that specialize in music and voiceovers and produce a few audiobooks as well. The huge move toward narrators producing their files in their own home recording studios has decimated the ranks of smaller studios producing audiobooks, but they are still out there.

The Specialty Publishers

There are important resources for blind, low vision, and dyslexic audiobook readers. The Library of Congress has the National

Library Service for the Blind and Physically Handicapped (NLS). NLS talking books are recorded by professional narrators in the studios of contractors who bid each year on book production. These contractors are usually nonprofit organizations that also provide other products and services for blind and physically handicapped individuals. Between the NLS recording studio in Washington, DC, and the contractor studios, NLS records more than one hundred titles per year.

Learning Ally, the American Foundation for the Blind (AFB), Talking Books, and the Royal National Institute of Blind People (RNIB) in Great Britain, produce audiobooks with volunteer narrators, especially textbooks which would not otherwise be commercially produced.

LibriVox volunteers read and record books in the public domain (books no longer under copyright, usually published before 1923), and make them available for free on the Internet.

Scholastic Audio, part of Scholastic, is the world's largest children's book publisher.

The 900-Pound Gorilla - ACX

The largest audiobook self-publisher is ACX (Audiobook Creation Exchange) an Amazon-owned company that makes audiobooks available on Audible, Amazon and iTunes.

Why did Amazon buy Audible and create ACX? *Because Amazon wants to sell more books in any format and recognizes the rising growth trajectory of audiobooks.*

There is a lot more about creating audiobooks with ACX ahead in Chapter 4, *Step-by-Step Guide to Amazon's ACX*, but first, let's take a look at doing it yourself.

Author Alert:
Do not create an
audiobook until you have
completed all edits in
the underlying book!

A *New York Times*
article on the growth
in the audiobook genre
of erotica described it as
"aural sex."

3

NARRATING YOUR OWN BOOK

© TheBookShepherd.com

Should You Be a "Do-It-Yourselfer?"

There are a few good reasons to narrate your own book, and as you will see, many more reasons why you should not.

Why you should:

1. *It's your book and your words, so you can tell your story best.* You know your

characters, your story or subject, and the thinking behind your words better than anyone else.

2. *You keep more money.* If you pay a narrator, you will either share royalties or pay them upfront to produce your audiobook. When you narrate your own book, your audiobook's royalty payments go to you (after your publisher or ACX takes a big chunk of it).

3. *You can be your own narrator* if:
   - You are a trained voice actor
   - You are a professional actor
   - You have a background in public speaking
   - You are a radio air talent or news anchor
   - You have read a lot of books for volunteer studios like Learning Ally and feel comfortable behind a microphone.

None of the above? Then get a professional to do it—please. It really is a lot harder than it looks. You could perform surgery on your own brain, but wow, what a mess!

Should You Narrate Your Book? Maybe ...

What if you have been told what a great voice you have? Having a good voice is a very small part of audiobook narration. Even experienced voice-over talent can struggle when they try the long-form audiobook narration format. Imagine a bunch of reviews on your book page complaining about the narrator. That's not something you want your readers to see.

OK, if you are going to go ahead and narrate your own book, here are some tips:

First, take the test created by top audiobook narrator (and one of my inspirations) Sean Pratt, who writes in his blog at *SeanPrattPresents.com*:

> *Set up a table and chair, along with a book or music stand, in some confined place in your home, i.e. a walk-in closet, alcove, or facing into the corner of a room. Put the book on the stand, grab a lamp or something to shine on the text, and then turn off any overhead light. What you're doing is mimicking what it's like to be in a sound booth.*
>
> *Now, read aloud for at least three hours a day for the next two weeks. If you stumble on a word, stop ... and begin that sentence again. If you come across a word, phrase, or person that you don't know and can't pronounce, stop ... go online and look it up*

... NO GUESSING! And don't just drone on and on, people! Your job is to entertain me, the listener, so keep up your energy, delivery and tempo. Got that? Good! That's the test.

Now that you've passed the test, listen to the playback. That will go a long way to tell you whether you should narrate your own book!

Narration Tricks of the Trade

- For fiction, listen to professionally-produced audiobooks in order to pick up on how audiobook narrators create great performances and emotional depth as they bring the words off the page.

- Unless you are paying a producer to be in the recording studio with you, you are entering the world of "directionless storytelling." Almost all audiobooks are now narrated by actors without directors.

- Showcase the story, NOT your voice. Stop trying to sound good. Don't try to be careful as you read, when the person you are trying to be is not being careful.

- Use an iPad or Android tablet. You can scroll quietly, see the words better in a dark reading environment, and there are built-in programs that allow you to add notes when absolutely necessary. Reading from your book or 400 pages of paper, creates many problems beyond killing trees.

- First, turning pages is noisy, and it's a noise that will need to be edited out of your recording. With paper pages you will be tempted to write lots of notes about emphasis or pronunciations. Looking at those notes while you read takes you "out of the words," and you won't be paying attention to the most important thing of all … telling the story!

Avoid the Phony Baloney Emphasis Syndrome (PBES)

Here is wonderful advice from one of my voice acting coaches, Paul Alan Ruben at *Paul-Alan-Ruben.com*, a Grammy award-winning voice acting coach and producer:

> *Phony exuberance—great for cheesy, cheerful, bouncy, plucky reads, not so good for being credible and a "non-salesperson" realistic delivery. You aren't always so happy, wide-eyed and amazed. You not only sound phony, you sound ignorant.*

> *Storytelling is by definition a performance art, a unique enterprise that deserves to be considered an artist's endeavor. How actors act fiction, and why authors can't possibly narrate their fiction as well as actors, is really meant to inform, and then persuade us to first imagine what it means to be an actor, so that we can imagine what it*

means to be a storyteller, so that, then, we can imagine what it means to be read to.

Accents

Ruben says nothing disrupts a compelling story more than a badly done accent:

Play the intent, not the accent. And if you even think you can't imitate a believable German accent, you're right. Don't go there.

For the accent challenged there's more than one way to sound 'foreign.' For example, slightly formalizing your English might be enough to suffice as an Asian accent. Finding a particular vowel sound that replicates a geographical region may be enough to keep the listener in willing suspension of disbelief.

Male/Female Voices

The Superpower studios use voice actors and actresses to voice the characters, which is probably not an option for you. So, unless you want to pay many times as much to have your audiobook produced, you will follow the standard practice of having one person voice all characters, no matter the gender, animal or alien voice required.

If you are giving it a try, then men, no falsettos; and women, no forced baritones. Don't be hammy. Play the traits that distinguish the opposite sex character. Focus on the tone, pacing, and attitude that distinguish each person. Then try a unique voice, not just a lower or breathier one.

Get an Acting Coach

Find a good acting coach, or even better, a voice acting coach, either locally or online. Check out the resource list at the end of this book.

An acting coach will help you:

- get emotionally connected

- narrate as if it is a symphony—high and low, up and down, fast and slow, loud and soft

- get out of your head and into the words

- be sincere, smile, and be physical

- relax, by practicing not to be afraid, and accepting there is one person, or maybe a few in a car listening to you—not thousands out there

- learn vocal exercises

Recording Studio Tips and Etiquette

For the highest quality narration, record in a local professional studio. Rates can be as low as $50 per hour of studio time or can run as high as $100-$200 per hour. It will take you up to two hours of recording time to get one finished recorded hour of narration.

Taylor Franklin, Managing Audio Engineer at
the Denver Media Center Recording Studios,
has some tips:

*One of the worst things a narrator can do in
the studio is to change something without
talking to the engineer. Everything is set up
a particular way. You might not realize it,
but moving a microphone just an inch or
two will change the sound quite a bit. On
top of that, if you tip over a $3,000 mic,
you are going to have a bad day.*

*I had a narrator in the studio that wanted
to stand, I always recommend sitting while
you read as long as you maintain good
posture. The narrator kept inching away
from the mic, by the time we were done he
had moved about three feet back! Slow
changes like this are hard to catch right
away, but they make a huge impact.*

Taylor adds that studio prep is key:

> *When you come into the studio, make sure you are rested and relaxed. Your job is to narrate and the engineer's job is to make you sound fantastic. Focus and consistency are key elements to a great audiobook.*

As a professional narrator, my own tips include:

- Make sure you eat a meal before you record, but no sooner than two hours before you start. Otherwise, the dreaded growling gurgling tummy rumbles will be the background track.

- Drink lots of water, preferably warm water up to two hours prior to recording. Sip water during breaks. Avoid coffee and strong teas. These can add lots of mouth clicks and smacks.

- For long recording days, hot tea with honey or "Throat Coat" brand tea can help soothe your throat post-recording.

Editing

You can have a professional edit the files
for you.

AudioBook producers talk in terms of "finished
hours." Finished hours are the actual running
time of the book after the final editing is
complete.

Because it can take two to four hours (or more)
to edit together a finished hour of audio, $25
to $75 per hour of actual editing time, or $50
to $100 per finished hour, the "finished hour"
methodology is not that expensive. If you
haven't edited your own audio, you can expect
a huge learning curve that requires at least
six hours to get one hour of audio.

Tech Stuff

There are minimum technical standards for
audiobooks. Amazon's ACX specs are minimums.
Please be aware that the major production

studios would not accept audio levels at ACX minimums. And guess what? Recording yourself on your iPhone or other Smartphone won't be good enough!

Your audiobook submitted to ACX must:

- be consistent in overall sound and formatting and be comprised of all mono (preferable) or all stereo files;

- include opening and closing credits and a retail audio sample that is between one and five minutes long;

- contain only one chapter/section that's shorter than 120 minutes and the section header must be read aloud;

- have room tone at the head and at the tail and be free of extraneous sounds;

- measure between -23dB and -18dB RMS and have -3dB peak values and a maximum -60dB noise floor; and

be a 192kbps or higher mp3, Constant
Bit Rate (CBR) at 44.1 kHz.

Is this all gibberish? That's a good reason to use
a professional audio editor or an experienced
narrator, who speaks in "decibel."

Creating Your Own Low-Cost Home Recording Setup

If you are going to record your own book, plan
to spend hundreds or thousands of dollars on
the necessary software and equipment. Let's
look at the **least expensive** basic ways to
produce your own audiobook.

The Basics

1. **A Good Microphone**
   Some microphones my fellow narrators
   recommend are the AT2020 USB,
   the Shure PG42 USB, and the Rode
   NT 1-A. Your built-in laptop, tablet,
   or smartphone microphones will

NOT generate high enough quality recordings. Want to know how you will sound? Some music stores, such as Guitar Center, will allow you to hear yourself on different mics you are considering.

2. **Recording Software**
   Sometimes called "Digital Audio Workstations," software can be found for free (Audacity for PC), for less than $20 (Apple's GarageBand) or for under $100 (TwistedWave for Macs or TwistedWave online for PCs). Each one has a learning curve!

3. **Recording Interface**
   If you have a higher quality condenser microphone, you will need a box that makes computers play nice with microphones. Inexpensive interfaces are made by Focusrite, Grace, Behringer and PreSonus.

4. **Tablet (Kindle, e-Reader, iPad)**
Reading off paper pages is the cheapest (but not cheap, when you consider the cost of ink and paper). It is much better to read a PDF or Word document off a tablet computer to cut down on noise. If you have excellent eyesight, you can even read off your smartphone.

5. **Acoustic Treatment**
You need to cut down background noise and sound reflections for a decent quality recording. If you are not going to spend thousands of dollars on a professional audio booth, try these alternatives:

- Moving blankets hung on curtain rods.

- Using a walk-in closet filled with sound-dampening clothes.

- Using a portable sound "booth" such as those made by sE Electronics, VocalBoothToGo, and Harlan Hogan's Porta-Booths.

None of these will be "sound proof," but you can get basic acceptable audio quality.

The fastest growing way people listen to audiobooks is on their smartphones.
(Audio Publishers Association)

STEP-BY-STEP GUIDE TO AMAZON'S ACX

ACX, the largest audiobook publisher of self-published books, is an Amazon company that produces books in the audiobook format. ACX makes audiobooks available on Audible, Amazon and iTunes.

STAGE ONE—REGISTERING YOUR BOOK ON ACX

1. Go to *ACX.com* and create an ACX account. You can use your existing Amazon email and password to log into ACX.

2. ACX displays possible book titles that match your title and name. Claim the best performing ISBN (International Standard Book Number) or version on Amazon. Many authors have more than one version of their book (e-book, paperback, hard cover), and ACX will pull in certain metadata from your Amazon listing, such as the summary and current rankings and ratings. Click on the "*This is my book*" tab.

3. The next choice you're given is to select how you want to make your book available. The options are:

- **I'm looking for someone to narrate and produce my audiobook.**
  This is by far the most popular option for authors. This is how you start searching for a qualified narrator to read and produce your book.

- **I have this book in audio and I want to sell it.**
  Choose this option if you have already recorded the book, but remember, it still has to meet ACX standards such as being in mp3 format, having the correct audio levels, and being edited into opening and closing credits and chapters. You must have a five minute long sample of the audiobook for retail sale.

● **I will narrate my own book and upload it later.**

The last option is to record your own audio and upload your book yourself.

4. You are presented with the *ACX Book Posting Agreement*, the legal contract you have to sign for your audiobook to be distributed through ACX. You certify you have the audio rights for your book, and (this is a biggie) that you will share the royalties with ACX and your narrator—if you have one—for seven years. So, if you end up with a huge seller, you will be splitting your royalties with the narrator for seven years. Yes, that's a long time, but realistically, few audiobooks will sell many copies past the first few years. If you update your book, you can re-submit it and begin the process again.

These are our terms. Please read and agree to continue...

VERSION 2.0

This ACX Book Posting Agreement ("Agreement") is a binding agreement between you, or the company or entity you represent, if you are entering into this Agreement on behalf of a company or entity ("you"), and Audible, Inc. ("Audible", "us" or "us"). It sets forth the terms you agree to when you make a book available for production as an audiobook on the audiobook production service and rights marketplace available at www.acx.com ("ACX") (any book you make available on ACX for production as an audiobook, a "Book"). You enter into this Agreement each time you make a Book available on ACX. That means that there is a separate Agreement between you and us for each Book you make available on ACX.

Among other things, in this Agreement you grant to us distribution rights in any audio recording of the Book that is completed through ACX (an "Audiobook") in the territory or territories you indicate (the "Territory") and the language you indicate (the "Language") when creating the title profile for your Book on ACX (the "Title

I have read the above ACX Book Posting Agreement and agree to its terms

Clicking "Agree & Continue" will mean that:

- You have the audio rights to the book.
- You want to add your book to ACX to get it produced as an audiobook.
- You will be able to meet potential narrators and producers for your book on ACX, and also may be contacted by audiobook publishers who may want to purchase the audio rights to your book (and then produce it off of the ACX system).
- You will distribute the completed audiobook, at minimum, through ACX's distribution channel (Amazon, Audible and iTunes).
- You will have the choice to distribute it on an exclusive or non-exclusive basis.
- Any information you put into your book's ACX title profile is accurate.

You have the option of a *"non-exclusive"* deal with ACX that allows you to sell your audiobook on CDs, from your website, or go through a separate distribution channel. In this scenario, you only get _25 percent of the royalties instead of the _40 percent you get when you give ACX exclusive distribution rights to sell your audiobook on Amazon, Audible and iTunes.

5. In ACX speak, you as author (or your publisher, if they have the audio rights) are known as the *Rights Holder*. The narrator you choose is the producer.

6. Where it asks for territory rights put in the regions in which you hold the copyright. The default response is "world." If you only hold rights for one country or territory, list that location instead.

7. Create your "title profile." This is the book description that will accompany your audiobook version on Amazon, Audible and iTunes. This profile is prepopulated for you with the information from your Amazon book page, but watch out, it occasionally mangles the formatting. You want a book description that's detailed and compelling to help narrators get excited about working on your project. Include some performance notes (characters, accents, overall tone, etc.) and mention if the title is part of a series i.e. *The Author's Guide to AudioBook Creation* (Book 2 in the *AuthorYOU Mini-Guide Series*).

8. Where it asks for copyright information, you are usually the copyright owner for the book and for the audiobook. Fill in this information along with the year of copyright.

Same yr as publish?

9. Next, you're asked if your book is fiction or nonfiction. Then you will be asked to select the one category that best describes your book. Go with the categories from your print version.

10. Next, you need to answer some general questions about the ideal narrator's voice you're looking for. Try to be as specific as possible when you're completing this section. Do you want a voice that's

"authoritative, masculine, engaging, feminine, sexy, urban, or inspirational?" Do you need an accent? Choosing correctly will save you from listening to a lot of auditions that totally miss the mark on what you want.

11. Use the *additional comments* section to mention your ranking on Amazon, how many books you sell monthly and weekly, and how you promote them. Help the narrators decide if the project will pay off for them or not.

12. The last step on this page is to upload your audition script. You can upload a file, preferably a Word document or PDF, or link to a URL where you have the audition script located. You don't have to upload your entire script. A good length is 2-3 pages, about five minutes of text. Include some dialog, some descriptive text, and any important accents or

character voices. If you can't find all of these things in one section, you can combine different passages in the audition script.

13. After you've uploaded your sample, click "OK" at the bottom of the page and you will be directed to the final page of information ACX needs to collect.

14. At the top of this page you're asked to type in how many words are in your book. When this is done, it can be estimated how many hours your final production will run. Be as accurate as possible, because if you do a "pay for production" deal, your cost will be based on the actual running time. Most word processing programs provide a word count for you. Microsoft Word, for example, displays this info in the bottom left hand corner of the document. If you are unable to get the word count

electronically, you can still do it the old-fashioned way. Pick a typical, full-text page of your book at random. Count the number of words in the top line of text, and then count the number of lines on the page. Multiply those two numbers. Then, multiply that number by the total number of pages in the book for your estimated total word count.

15. You need to provide your tax and bank information in order to be paid. You can't move forward with your book until this information is entered.

16. Next, select how you want to be paid royalties, either by check or direct deposit to your bank.

STAGE TWO—THE DEAL WITH THE NARRATOR

Decide how you want to pay for your production. Do you want to pay your producer upon completion of the audiobook (a fee per finished hour, as part of a Pay for Production deal), or do you prefer to split your royalties with them 50-50 (as part of a Royalty Share deal)? There are a few choices:

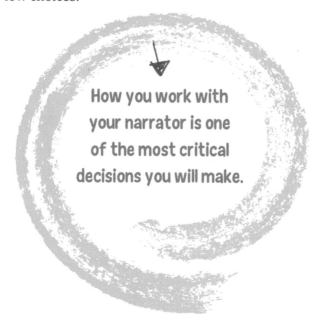

How you work with
your narrator is one
of the most critical
decisions you will make.

acx navigation: About ACX | How it Works | Promote Yourself | Need Help? | Search

How would you like to pay for the audiobook's production?

You can pay the producer a per-finished-hour fee (Pay For Production) or you can simply share royalties with them (Royalty Share). If you are unsure at this time you can click both options, but the more specific that you are, the more likely you are to find the right Producer for you. You can always change your mind; you don't need to commit 100% until you are ready to make a formal offer to one of the Producers you find on ACX. To learn more about these two options, please check out the What's the Deal? section.

Choose one or both below:*

☑ Royalty Share (50-50 share of royalties earned)

50-50 share of royalties earned. By choosing this method of payment, you will be paid monthly to ACX based on half of royalties earned each time the audiobook sells. This limits your potential revenue, but also limits your risk. Learn more.

Distribution will be EXCLUSIVE distribution on Amazon, Audible, and iTunes™

(40% royalty) Why does it have to be exclusive?

☑ Pay for Production

I'll pay: $ [Unspecified ▼] Per finished hour
(2.2 hrs @ $0 - $0 hr = $0.00 - $0.00)

- *You can make an offer to a narrator to produce your audiobook.* Do this by making them a cash offer based on the length of the audiobook. You are paying for the entire production—narration, editing, and mastering of the files for upload on ACX.

- *You can offer a royalty split.* That means the narrator agrees to produce the audiobook without charging you a fee. Instead, the narrator will get 50 percent of your royalty payments for seven years.

- *You can negotiate with the narrator for a hybrid deal.* This would include paying a fixed amount upfront, plus splitting the royalties.

Author Alert:

This is one of the most critical decisions you will make. It will greatly determine how much money you will make from your audiobook, so here are details for each option.

Pay for Production

You pay a narrator to produce the audiobook for you, and in return you receive all royalties earned from sales of your audiobook. If you choose this option you can enter the amount you are willing to pay per finished hour (PFH). The usual rate is $100 to $400 per finished hour. If you want an experienced narrator, you will probably be in the $200 PFH and above range.

Narrators spend an average of three to four hours to record, edit and master one hour of audio. So if you pay $200 per completed hour, they are earning as little as $50 per work hour.

Narration Rates

- Inexperienced - $100 per finished hour or royalty share

- Moderately experienced - $150 to $200 per finished hour

- Very Experienced - $200 to $400+ per finished hour

- SAG-AFTRA union narrators get a minimum of $225 per finished hour

If you choose to pay up-front for production and place your book on ACX, you will pocket 40 percent of the royalties from each audiobook sold; the other 60 percent goes to ACX. For this deal, if you pay the narrator a great rate up front for really good work, just like the big publishing houses do, you reap a much bigger share of the sale price of each book.

Royalty Share

The narrator covers the entire cost of the production, including recording, editing and mastering the book to ACX standards. When your audiobook is sold, you split your share of the royalties 50/50 with the narrator. ACX still gets 60 percent of the royalties, so you are actually splitting the remaining 40 percent with the narrator. Yes, that's 20 percent of the book sales price for each of you.

Most experienced narrators will not audition for Royalty Share only deals. Unless you have an established or potential bestselling book on Amazon, many narrators will not risk absorbing all the up-front production costs. If a book is ranked as number one million plus in sales on Amazon, it is getting roughly one sale per year. You will get few, if any, auditions.

Stipends

ACX offers to pay the $100 per finished hour bonus called a "stipend" to narrators on titles ACX determines are attractive enough to sell many copies. ACX pays this stipend, not the author! Which books are eligible for a stipend is not a decision made by a human. ACX uses an algorithm to determine which books are eligible based on sales of the print versions, ratings, reviews, the book length (longer is better), whether it's part of a series and more. The actual formula used is not made public. It really is ACX's "secret formula."

To qualify for a Stipend payment from ACX:

- Titles must be royalty share.
- Titles must usually be open for audition for two to three weeks in order for ACX to determine if a stipend is warranted.
- Titles must be completed within 60 days of the producer's acceptance of the offer, so production is on a fast track.

Hybrid Deal

How about a win-win option for both the author and narrator? You can pay a smaller per finished hour rate and a royalty share. This helps narrators cover their costs. A $100 per finished hour payment plus the 20 percent royalty share will get you many more auditions.

Here are the steps once you have decided how you want to pay the narrator:

1. Click Save & Continue to move to the final page. This page summarizes your information and gives you the option to post your book's information to ACX and start receiving auditions.

2. You can also search ACX for narrators to invite to audition. Do you want a male or female narrator? Think about the voice you heard in your head when you wrote your book. If your story can be told by a man or a woman, you can choose "either" in your Title Profile.

3. If you have already chosen a narrator, you can go to the narrator's profile. Make sure you add a note on the "Audition" page, saying "I have already selected a narrator for this title" so you don't get deluged with unnecessary auditions.

4. Make an offer! Clicking this button will start the process of making an agreement or deal.

STAGE THREE-PRODUCING THE AUDIOBOOK

Congratulations, you now have a partner in telling your story. Your next steps are:

1. Set a production schedule based on your needs and the narrator's availability.

2. The first benchmark is when the "First 15 Minutes" are due. It is reasonable to give your narrator 10 days to two weeks to produce and post the first 15 minutes of your audiobook. This is your

opportunity to ask for changes in the delivery style or character voices.

Once you click on the button to accept the first 15 minutes, your contract with the narrator is in force. There are cancellation penalties called "kill fees" you are required to pay the narrator if you have approved the first 15 minutes and later decide not to go through with your agreement.

If you are really unhappy with how your audiobook is sounding, this is your chance to cancel the agreement by notifying ACX you would like to choose a different narrator.

3. The "Finished Audiobook Due Date" is the date you require the narrator to be finished with production. This time will vary depending on the length and complexity of your book (lots of characters, many foreign words and accents). It may

take two to three months for the narrator to finish the book. Make sure to include time to review your final audio and communicate any corrections ("pickups") to your narrator.

4. You are also responsible for uploading an audiobook book cover image (2500 x 2500 pixels, square). Note that your cover image for your hardcover, paperback or e-book will NOT meet the ACX audiobook standards. ACX requires it to be big and square. At this writing, there are no exceptions.

STAGE FOUR–REVIEW, APPROVE and PAY

Almost there!

1. Request clear and specific corrections to the final audio as necessary. It's good to review chapters as they are posted rather than wait until the entire book is ready to upload to ACX. The narrator

expects to fix mispronounced or skipped words, technical glitches and extraneous sounds like a dog bark or siren in the background. Remember that this is a shared vision of your book. Your characters might not sound the same as they did in your head. Voice actors should be able to make creative choices.

2. As soon as you approve the edits, the narrator will press the "I'm Done" button.

Do you approve this audiobook?

By clicking Yes, I Approve, (a) I confirm that I listened to the completed audiobook and that the audiobook meets the terms set forth in the ACX Audiobook Production Standard Terms that I entered into with the Producer and the specifications set forth in the ACX Rules for Audiobook Production, (b) I am approving the audiobook for upload to ACX and distribution by Audible, and (c) I understand that distribution by Audible will only occur after the Producer confirms through ACX that the Producer has received payment.

Note: This is also your final opportunity to change the name that will appear in the "Publisher" field on the Audible.com product listing. The published by name is typically the name of the actual ACX rights holder or corresponding company name. If you are satisfied with the existing name AND you are ready to confirm that you are completed with your audiobook, you can simply click "Yes, I approve"

Richard Rieman

Yes, I approve. No, not yet

3. When you press the "Approved" button, payment is due on "Pay for Production" (not Royalty Share) titles. When paid for the production, the narrator must press the "I've Been Paid" button to get to the next step.

4. Approve and pay for your audiobook (unless it is a Royalty Share). The final payment amount is calculated by ACX based on the final length of the audiobook.

Congratulations! This audiobook production is complete
Now, once it passes validation, we'll sell the audiobook through our retail partners, Audible.com, Amazon.com and iTunes. While you wait, you may want to visit the Promote Yourself section to learn about social media marketing.

5. Your title will then be submitted to ACX to receive a quick technical quality check and, if all is well, your audiobook goes into "Ready for Retail" status. From that point, your audiobook should be available for sale within 10 to 21 business days of your approval.

GIVING YOUR BOOK A VOICE

© TheBookShepherd.com

There are right ways and wrong ways to find the voice actor who will bring your words to life. Choosing the wrong track to go down will ensure failure for your audiobook.

I've had the opportunity to work with many of the professional narrators who consistently produce excellent audiobooks.

The 10 Best Ways to Find the Right Narrator

Teri Schnaubelt, narrator extraordinaire at *TeriSchnaubelt.com,* believes these are the best ways to give your book a voice. Teri and Jeffrey Kafer at *JeffreyKafer.com*, share these top ten tips for finding the perfect voice for you:

Teri's Top Ten Tips:

1. *Listen to samples on ACX, then investigate some of the narrators whom you like.*

2. *Check out narrator reviews on Audible. Do they consistently get good/great reviews? How many books have they done?*

3. *Are the narrators also actors? Being an actor helps with creating characters as well as understanding the art of storytelling.*

4. *Are they working as narrators part-time or full-time?*

5. *Feel free to ask for references from other authors who have used the narrators you are considering.*

6. *Ask the narrators if they use a professional editor or if they do the work themselves.*

7. *Ask them what kind of turnaround time you could expect if you hired them for your project.*

8. *You don't always need an audition. If they have done books in a similar genre, you can often tell how great they would be without having them audition for your specific book.*

9. *If you're new to the audiobook production world, do your due diligence by doing some research on ACX, and then ASK QUESTIONS if you don't understand the process or what's involved.*

10. *Audiobook narrators read your book as it is written. You may need to make some changes in the text to make it friendlier to the ear, which keeps the listener in the moment. For instance, if your printed book says "you're reading this book," you might change the verb to be "you're listening to this book."*

Your narrator is your partner. Communicate your expectations from the beginning of the relationship.

The 10 Worst Ways to Find a Narrator

Here is what **NOT** to do. Jeffrey Kafer at *JeffreyKafer.com* and I agree you will run into problems getting a good narrator if you:

1. **Have a Poor Cover**
You CAN judge a book by its cover. If your book cover looks amateurish, royalty share narrators will not want to audition, because they don't think the audiobook version will sell very many copies.

2. **Ask for a Royalty Split on a Book that Isn't Selling**
If you have only 3 reviews on Amazon and your sales rank is 2,395,763, than 20% of zero is still zero. Or, it's worse than zero for your narrator if it's a 10 hour book that takes 50 or 60 hours to produce.

3. **Require Music or Sound Effects**

   Only the big publishers with big budgets include any sound effects in highly produced "audio dramas." If you require any music, be prepared to pay extra for the rights and for an engineer or producer to add it.

4. **Ask for Both Male and Female Narrators**

   When you request "co-narrators," you are either going to double your cost for a pay for production deal or ask two narrators to accept half the usual royalties. It really is accepted practice for audiobooks (traditionally and self-published) to have one voice do all the characters, whether male, female, animal, or alien.

5. **Ask for a 20 Minute Long Audition**

   You will probably know within the first 30 seconds whether a narrator is right for your book. A 5 minute long audition that includes a couple character voices will do.

6. **Require Multiple Accents**

Having a British and French character should not be a problem for most experienced narrators. But, adding German, Russian, Irish and more international voices into your book will shrink your pool of narrators into a tiny pond. Especially with secondary characters, perfect accents should not be expected.

7. **Make the E-book Free on a Royalty Share Book**

Who is going to pay for the audiobook if you are giving the e-book away? You should offer a pay for production deal.

8. **Have a Very Short Book**

The term "book" is used here very loosely. $100 per finished hour "books" that are really 10-minute long articles end up paying less than $17 to the narrator. Books should be at least 10,000 words (more than an hour) long to have an audio version.

9. **Have a Badly Edited Book**

Lots of misspellings, words that don't mean what you think they do, poor grammar, or having characters change names (continuity errors) will make a narrator regret having his or her name on your book.

10. **Don't Communicate with Your Narrator**

You and your narrator are partners in in the production of the audiobook. Don't be a silent partner. Respond quickly to questions and requests. Stay engaged through the entire process.

6

GOING OUTSIDE AMAZON'S ACX

Amazon's ACX is by far the biggest self-publisher of audiobooks, but it's not the only way to record your own book or find a narrator. Even if you go through ACX, you may want to do a "non-exclusive" agreement so you can sell your audiobook on other platforms.

The World Beyond ACX

- The APA (Audio Publishers Association) at *AudioPub.org* has a great resource list of audiobook publishers and narrators, including Brilliance, Blackstone, and Deyan Audio studios previously mentioned.

- WOVO, the World Voices Organization, runs *VoiceOver.biz*, where some of the top professional audiobook narrators can be found outside ACX.

- *AudioFile Magazine* at *AudioFileMagazine.com* also has an audiobook talent and industry guide for finding narrators, studios and more.

- You can still produce your audiobook on CDs through a plethora of CD creation services, even as digital downloads become the more popular choice. The largest CD duplication companies include

CD Baby, Kunaki and Disc Makers. Some services will handle storage and shipping of the CDs. You handle the sales to your fans off your website and at author events.

Audiobooks
are ideal
as builders of
your email lists.

Selling Outside ACX/Amazon/Audible/iTunes

AudioBooks.com is a recent entry into the self-publishing environment, aiming to be what Smashwords is to audiobooks. *AudioBooks.com* has created an audiobook distribution service called "*Author's Republic*" which allows self-published authors to sell audiobooks through more than a dozen distributors and retailers.

Author's Republic is a publishing aggregator that submits titles to *Audiobooks.com*, Audible, iTunes, Amazon, B.N.com, Scribd, Downpour, and *tunein*, as well as library providers such as Overdrive. Most of these platforms will pay authors an average 35 percent royalty share. Audible, iTunes and Amazon will pay a 25 percent "non-exclusive" royalty. Author's Republic does not require the seven year commitment that ACX does. They offer a six-month "out."

NOTE: If you use Author's Republic, you must have a "non-exclusive" agreement with ACX to be able to still distribute your audiobook on Amazon, Audible and iTunes. You will get a 25 percent instead of 40 percent royalty share on those platforms. If you are splitting your ACX royalties with a narrator, your title will NOT be eligible for Author's Republic.

- OverDrive at *OverDrive.com* is a platform that distributes audiobooks to libraries. OverDrive is very selective of the authors it chooses to include in its platform with audiobooks usually coming from the "Superpower" traditional publishing companies. You should have a track record of success before you try to get into the OverDrive catalog.

- Barnes & Noble has a NOOK Audiobook App available for iPhone and iPad. *NOOKAudiobooks.com* is offering more than 60,000 audiobooks online, which can be listened to via any NOOK by Samsung tablet, iPhone, iPad or Android device via the app. The app allows customers to purchase the audiobook through the app without a subscription.

- *Audiobooks.com* is the second largest audiobook subscription service also with more than 60,000 audiobooks online. This company is also very choosy about which titles are included in its library.

- Downpour at *Downpour.com* is the next largest subscription service, and its library is almost exclusively bestsellers. Once again, it is a pretty exclusive club even though the site rents tens of thousands of audiobook titles.

Giving Your AudioBooks Away

You may be more interested in using audiobooks as a lead generator than as a separate source of income. Posting your audio for free is one way to steer potential readers to purchase your print and e-book versions.

Australian science fiction and fantasy author Adam Train at *TranscendentTales.com* releases his audiobooks for free on SoundCloud and YouTube in "podcast" format.

Adam Train rides the "*podiobook*" train:

I decided to go the free route because I feel that the 'direct payment' model, particularly for digital content, is an antiquated one. In the digital realm, if people want your content and don't want to pay for it, there is almost always a way they can obtain it through piracy or simply by sharing it. This along with the fact that as an unknown writer it is tough enough to get people to read or listen to your work, let alone if they have to pay for it, making it free is marketing unto its self.

Because my focus for the works is to produce them into an audiobook podcast and 99% of podcasts are free, it also made it an easy choice. Most importantly, as a consumer of digital content myself, I would rather consume free content and be given the option to support or donate. Not to mention that today there are countless ways to monetize content via indirect or passive means, i.e. sponsors, merchandise and crowdfunding just being a few.

This entire creative endeavor is more about fulfilling a lifelong dream to bring my series of stories to life. I would be beyond happy if I made enough money to tell stories for a living and make enough from my works to produce more works. I hope to build enough subscribers and listeners to utilize advertising as most podcasters do, and I also have a Patreon (crowdfunding) account and PayPal donations account and hope to grow these like many others have.

Where Adam Train has chosen to give his audiobooks away in general, you could do a variation. Such as:

- Give away free for a limited time.
- Give it away as a bonus when purchasing the e-book edition.

- Include it in your overall launch strategy—bringing the listeners back to your website to initiate the download requires them to leave their email address.

- Create a "build your email list" campaign from your Home page on your website: "Get my latest book for 30 days free: Subscribe here."

When you use an audiobook as a Free Bonus Offer from your website, the capturing of listener's emails allows you to stay in contact— from announcements to your latest ventures to offering special deals, webinars and workshops.

In China,
digital materials are
expected "to be free."
Chinese media powerhouse
Sina.com says only 19 percent
of the users it polled would
be willing to pay for
audiobooks.

Making Your AudioBook Profitable

© TheBookShepherd.com

The sad truth is that you don't have control over your audiobook sale price once you sign up with a retail distributor. However, the good news is that even when the retail price is discounted, your royalty share is usually based on the retail price you originally posted. However, sometimes, special sales may lower your royalties.

How Much Will Your AudioBook Sell For?

The regular audiobook price on Amazon, Audible and iTunes is generally priced based on its length as follows:

- Under 1 hour: less than $7
- 1 – 3 hours: $7 - $10
- 3 – 5 hours: $10 - $20
- 5–10 hours: $15 - $25
- 10–20 hours: $20 - $30

Of course, depending on your expertise, celebrity, even the demand, the price will vary.

How Much Will You Make?

If you are the ACX "Rights Holder" selling *exclusively* through Amazon, Audible and iTunes and sharing royalties with the

"Producer," you will each get 20 percent of the sale price. For example, if your title sells for $20, you will get $4 per sale. If you chose a "Pay for Production" deal, you will get a 40 percent royalty share, or $8 per sale.

Shorter books make it easy to pay up front and keep the 40 percent share. If you pay $400 to a narrator to produce a two hour long book, you only need to sell 100 copies to break even! If you decided on a *non-exclusive* deal through ACX, you receive a 25 percent royalty share. With the non-exclusive choice, splitting royalties with a narrator is not an option, so you must pay for production.

Crowdfunding Your Audiobook

The best source of crowdfunding information for authors is Dr. Judith Briles' *The CrowdFunding Guide for Authors & Writers.*

Judith Briles is the author of 35 books and one of the nation's top book shepherds. She believes authors can fund their books (if the content is compelling enough) through general funding sites such as *KickStarter.com* and *Pledge.com*. Author specific sites include *IndieGoGo.com*, *Upspringer.com* and *GoFundMe.com*, all of which help a wide range of musicians, writers, filmmakers and other creative types.

> You have your hat
> in hand ... you are asking
> for money. What's going
> to 'seduce' the donor? What's
> the aha? What's the benefit
> for the completed book
> to the reader?

Tips from Dr. Briles include:

Kickstarter.com does a huge number of books ... but again, there is a BUT—it does not support 'causes' or a charity. It's the gorilla in the playground and has funded more than $20,000,000 in literary projects last year alone.

Where IndieGoGo, and Upspringer welcome authors, Kickstarter can be picky. Groucho Marx said he would never join a club that would have him as a member. Groucho would have had a much easier time getting into IndieGoGo. They take almost everybody. Keep that in mind.

Is your project worth it? Really ... is it worth it? Be honest. Is this an ego thing ... or is your story, your how-to/solution new with a twist? Does it have a WOW to it? Is it interesting? If you can't honestly say yes, yes, yes and yes, the odds are that you are going to struggle with getting funding. If people—your family and friends included—can't get excited, do you expect perfect strangers to?

You have your hat in hand ... you are asking for money. What's going to 'seduce' the donor? What's the aha ... what's the benefit for the completed book to the reader ... what will the donor get in return—yes, feeling good in supporting you ... but is there anything else (great rewards count here as well)? People will want to know how you will use their money; what they will get in return; and yes, that you are a good steward in moving the project forward.

The key here is to include the funds you will need to produce your audiobook when you create your book campaign. That means targeting an extra $3,000 or so, depending whether you plan to pay for production or use a recording studio and editor if you self-narrate.

8

Promoting Your AudioBook

With audiobook in hand, your promo hat comes into play. You have a new product that needs to be shouted out to your fans and the listener/reader world that you have already identified. It all involves engagement, especially in the social media world.

Now I will share my dozen "must dos":

12 Ways to Go into "Promo Mode"

1. Create a post on your blog. You have one, right? Include a book cover image and an audio sample. The "retail sample" required by ACX is ideal for this post. Don't forget to include a "live" link for the reader to"go-go-go" to.

2. Post a status update on Facebook, and any other social media that you post on. Link to your book page at Amazon or directly to your Audible or iTunes audiobook page.

3. Email and Tweet about your audiobook going on sale. Respond to or Retweet any commentary you receive.

4. Ask key peers and colleagues if they would help share the news by emailing and posting about your book. Better yet, create the posts and Tweets so all they have to do is copy, paste and post. You

will get more success and support if
you do.

5. Request listener reviews from all your
    contacts. Buy the book for them, if
    necessary.

6. Link your Audible reviews back to your
    Author Page on Amazon and post on
    your website with the appropriate links.

7. Add a link or "Buy Now" graphic to your
    website and blog so that people can buy
    your audiobook with one click.

8. Participate in webinars, use Google+
    Hangouts, Periscope, Blabs and Twitter
    chats to reach the online audience.
    Promote the audio version as if it's a
    completely new book.

9. Interview your narrator. Have a Google+
    Hangout with the person who recorded
    your book. This is great publicity for

both of you. Then create a blog around the interview—double linking it: to YouTube for the interview and to Amazon to buy the audiobook.

10. Create a promotional video. A book trailer is an essential tool in the overall book marketing plan. According to ComScore, a video trailer can increase the chance of a potential reader buying your book by 64 percent. You can engage a Trailer expert or use a resource like *Animoto.com* for less than $100.

11. Send colleagues and reviewers a synopsis or a code for a free copy of your audiobook (more about that on the next page).

12. With future books, try to time your audiobook release with the print and e-book versions, so all of your efforts can simultaneously share your promotion efforts. Make sure you mention all formats in all you do.

Reviews are essential to "move" your audiobook. Take advantage of the promotional codes that ACX gives you.

Bounties

Encourage your audience to buy your book as a new Audible Listener member on *Audible.com*. Audible wants you to help them get new members subscribing at $14.95 per month. That's almost $180 per year, so Audible is willing to pay you to bring your fans into the mix. A new Audible customer gets a free book as part of a 30-day trial. When you tell your readers about the book, encourage them to visit a link that will prompt them for the trial. If they select your book as a free trial and stay with the membership for 61 days, you'll earn a bounty on your royalty statement.

In a royalty share deal, ACX will split the $50 bounty between you and your narrator ($25 each), which is still more than any other audiobook sale you can make.

NOTE: Unfortunately, at this writing, bounty payments are not allowed in six states, including Arkansas, Colorado, Missouri, Maine, Rhode Island, and Vermont. This is due to some states considering bounties a prohibited sales incentive.

Promotional or "Gift" Codes

Audible has another program to help boost your sales. You can get 25 free download codes for each of your books. ACX usually sends you the codes when your audiobook goes on sale, but if you don't get an email from ACX, you need to request them through *Support@ACX.com*.

> **Use the codes to GIFT the book ... ensuring the person getting the code is listening to YOUR book.**

You can distribute these codes to drive reviews and sales of your audiobook. The best thing is you still receive royalties for each book downloaded with the free code, and you receive a bounty if the purchase is eligible for one.

No Co

This would be an ideal way to shout out about
your audiobook:

**Get my new audiobook free with a
30-day trial via *Audible.com***

Warning: If you just send people the promotional codes, they can use them to buy ANY title,
not just yours. It is better to use the codes to
GIFT the audiobook ... ensuring the person
getting the code is listening to YOUR book.

To gift your audiobook, "buy" it yourself, with
one of the codes, and send it to the email
address of the listener. Go to the title, select
"send as a gift" and add it to your cart, fill out
the gift form with your message, a thank you
card, and the listener's email address. Check
out, and select "Have a promo code" and apply.
Click the "use credit" next to the book name,
and apply it. Complete the purchase for "$0.00"
and you have now "gifted" your audiobook in
exchange for a review.

AudioBook Blast

How do you get the most bang for your promotional code buck? Try "Audiobook Blast" at *AudiobookBlast.com/authors* to give away your ACX codes to interested listeners. Every Tuesday morning an email is sent to a couple of thousand audiobook listeners. You gift them a code in exchange for an unbiased review of your audiobook on Audible, Amazon or Goodreads for $10 per title. You can also promote a sale or a *Whispersync* deal on your combination e-book/audiobook bundle for $5.

Facebook Promotions

You can ask for reviews in exchange for a free audiobook download in a few Facebook groups, including:

- *AudiobookJungle*
- *FreeAudioBookGiveaways*
- *FreeAudible*

Best Promotional Advice from Experienced AudioBook Authors

Acclaimed Voice-Over Actor, Coach and Film and TV Actor David H. Lawrence XVII of *vo2gogo.com* and *ACXMasterClass.com* says some authors are getting great audiobook advice from their writing coaches:

> *Authors are being told to write with audio in mind. Creating characters that leap off the page is one thing, but creating characters that will also sound good will help tell a better story, and provide a better experience for the listener. That means more sales, since the actual writing itself will be better.*
>
> *They're also learning to put the retail sample of the book everywhere, and not just allowing it to live on Amazon, Audible and iTunes. Putting their samples on their own websites, on themed and review sites,*

on sites that deal with the subject matter they've written about, even on fan sites, leads to more exposure, and more sales. And authors are being taught to promote not only their written books, but anywhere they link to their Amazon hardback or paperback editions, to also add their audiobook links.

One of my author's coaches said, 'Never give away your IP.' IP, in this case, means 'intellectual property.' Meaning, pay narrators a great rate up front for really good work, just like the big publishing houses do, and then reap 100 percent of the reward on the back end for yourself.

Start drafting your audiobook marketing plan as soon in the process as possible. Keep your fans up to date throughout the production process to build anticipation for your audiobook. Your audiobook marketing plans can help you set due dates for your production and the timeline for producing your audiobook and putting it up for sale.

Just like your print or e-book, the audiobook is your baby. Announce it with the same enthusiasm you would if you were celebrating a birth. Don't miss out. Become part of the AudioBook Revolution!

AudioBook Resources

© TheBookShepherd.com

Additional audiobook resources for authors are always welcome. Below are some of my favorites:

Blogs

Subscribe to Narrator Karen Commins' excellent blog at *blog.KarenCommins.com* for news and features for both authors and narrators.

Social Media

- *Twitter*: Karen Commins also has the best Twitter resources in her updated lists of audiobook publishers, narrators and bloggers at *twitter.com/KarenCommins/lists*

- *Facebook Groups* include the AudioBook Community, a forum for all audiobook listeners to discover audiobooks and connect with other fans, publishers, authors, and narrators. ACX Narrators and Producers is a group filled with narrators looking for books to record and lots of good advice on audiobook production.

- *LinkedIn*: AudioBook Narrators and AudioBook Industry Professionals are two very good groups to find narrators and advice.

Equipment

Sweetwater.com is a great resource for both audio equipment and software specifically for audiobook and voiceover production.

Technical Advice

Some of the best recording tips are those from "Alex the Audio Scientist" at *blog.ACX.com*.

ACX Cover Specs

- Images must be no smaller than 2400 x 2400 pixels in size. That's huge!

- The resolution of these images can be no smaller than 72 dpi and at least 24-bit.

- Images must be squared. The squared cover must be a true squared cover and cannot be rectangular with colored borders on the side, like a CD case cover.

- Images can not refer to physical CDs or media other than the audio presented.

- Pornographic and offensive materials are not allowed.

- Image types allowed are JPEG, TIFF or PNG.

- Each image should be labeled as the full title, such as **Book_title.jpg** or **ISBN number.jpg.**

- Images must contain both the name of the title and author.

Check out *RRVoice.com* for Resource Updates.

Video and Audio Promo Production

You can create your own video book trailer using a clip from your audiobook with the tools at *Animoto.com* and post them on SoundCloud, YouTube and audioBoom.

The Storytellers

Just a special few—listen to them if you want examples of your words from incredibly talented storytellers:

Jim Dale	Barbara Rosenblat
Simon Vance	Katherine Kellgren
Scott Brick	Kate Rudd
Davina Porter	Sophie Thompson
Bernard Cribbens	Tavia Gilbert
Khristine Hvam	Juliet Stevenson

Resources come and go. Make sure you follow my Blog on my website, *RRVoice.com*, for ongoing, updated resources.

You can also follow me on:

 twitter.com/RichardRieman

 facebook.com/AudiobookCreation/

©TheBookShepherd.com

12 Bonus Tips for an Author's AudioBook Success

1. A really good audiobook can boost the sales of your print and digital editions. The best example is Andy Weir's *The Martian*, narrated by R.C. Bray. It was an unknown self-published book until the audio edition hit the Audible Top 10. A big publishing contract and the Matt Damon movie soon followed.

2. Decide whether Amazon (ACX) exclusivity is your best strategy. You will make 15% more in royalty share if you sign the 7-year ACX exclusivity agreement, but you will lose the 35% royalty shares available from Barnes and Noble, *Audiobooks.com* and other distributors through Author's Republic.

3. The cheapest way to get your audiobook produced is by sharing royalties with a narrator. You will get 20% of each audiobook's price. But, if your audiobook is a big seller, you will regret not having the 40% royalty share on ACX or 25-35% through Author's Republic if you had chosen to pay your narrator for production up front.

4. If you are going to narrate your own book, make sure you have the time, the energy, and the technical help you will need to get it done.

5. Use SoundCloud to create audio clips for your promotion. Your ACX contract allows you to share as much as 15 minutes, so take at least the first five minutes or the first chapter and load it onto the *SoundCloud.com* audio platform for free.

6. Treat the launch of your audiobook the same way you launch the other formats. Promote it on social media and do interviews. Your "emerging children" deserve as much attention as your first!

7. Add links to both the Audible and iTunes versions of your audiobooks to all of your author's pages, including your website—and Author Central page on Amazon.

8. Mention that you have audiobooks whenever you do an interview or talk about your books and build your email list with everyone who buys your audiobook.

9. On your Goodreads author page, add the audiobook edition on Goodreads for each of your books. There is a link on the title page to add a new edition.

10. If you have an Amazon Advantage account, make sure your audiobook appears on your book page. The Author Central team can be helpful if you have trouble with getting the links to appear.

11. Consider using your audiobook as a "free bonus" when they buy your book, and vice versa!

12. Listen to bestselling audiobooks in your genre, so you can decide the kind of narrator that can really bring voice to your words.

Read to your children, so they will grow up with an appreciation of how a storyteller uses his or her voice to bring words to life.
— **Richard Rieman**

Acknowledgments

I am especially thankful to "The Book Shepherd" Judith Briles, my guide on the journey to becoming an author. I am grateful that Judith has included me in her *AuthorYOU Mini-Guide Series*. And that's why the "sheepies" are part of this book.

I am so lucky to have been guided into voiceovers and audiobook narration by some of the top professionals in the business, including Melissa Leebaert, Sean Pratt, Pat Fraley, Paul Alan Ruben, David Lawrence XVII, Dan O'Day, and Bill DeWees.

I am grateful to Taylor Franklin of Denver Media Center studios for his technical skill, Karen Souer for her audio editing help, John Maling of *Editing by John* for his editing skills, Don Sidle for the illustrations and Nick Zelinger for the cover and layout.

None of us can be creative without personal inspiration. Mine comes from my best friend Scott Brockmeier, my children Sean, Shannon and Erin, and most of all, my partner in life, Nancy Hinde.

Finally, this book is dedicated to the warm, fun and friendly community of authors and voice actors.

About the Author

With smiling Irish eyes and a rich, warm voice to match, Richard Rieman (rhymes with "demon") is an audiobook narrator, creator and coach specializing in helping first-time audiobook authors and rights holders. Richard has narrated dozens of titles on Amazon, Audible, iTunes and YouTube, including Steve Snyder's *SHOT DOWN*, Nancy Geise's *Auschwitz 34207*, Charles Clark's *The Bootlegger '40 Ford*, and Bruce Comstock's *A Life in the Air*. He also produces audiobooks for authors voicing their own audiobooks, including Judith Briles' *The CrowdFunding Guide for Authors & Writers*.

Before his audiobook adventures, Richard was a news anchor and reporter at the RKO Radio Networks in NYC, WTOP in Washington, DC, and WLS and WMAQ Radio in Chicago.

WORKING WITH RICHARD

Richard Rieman speaks to a variety of
author groups and organizations
on creating audiobooks.

Contact him for speaker availability at
Richard@RRVoice.com
for narration services or consulting on
your audiobook project.